MEGA RESCUERS

picthall and gunzi

Created & produced by:
Picthall & Gunzi Limited
21A Widmore Road
Bromley
BR1 1RW
United Kingdom

Designer: Paul Calver
Written and edited by: Christiane Gunzi and Chez Picthall
Editorial assistant: Katy Rayner
Vehicle consultant: Gary Boyd-Hope

Hardback ISBN **978-1-905503-42-1**

Reproduction in Singapore by Colourscan
Printed & bound in China by WKT Company Ltd

**Picthall & Gunzi would like to thank the following companies
and individuals for the use of their images:**
AgustaWestland; American Emergency Vehicles, Jefferson, NC; All Wales
Ambulance Services; Automobili Lamborghini SpA; Chrysler Group; Don
Winslow Photography (www.donwinslow.net); Flying Tankers Inc.; Gerard
Donnelly; Getty Images; Iveco Group; J Godwin/Emergency Vehicles
Online (www.emergency-vehicles.co.uk); Jige International; John Dennis
Coachbuilders Ltd; Kris Walker, Oceanid; Leavesley All Terrain Emergency
Response Vehicle (ATERV) – Leavesley International – www.leavesley-
international.com; Mader International Pty Ltd – Australian Ambulance
and Specials Vehicle Manufacturer – www.mader.com.au; Maritime and
Coastguard Agency; Metalcraft Marine Inc. and City of Seward, Alaska;
Michael Martinelli; Mike Evans; Oshkosh Truck Corporation;
RNLI/Nicholas Leach and Graeme Sweeney; Scania Image Desk; Steve
Bailey, Gibbs Technologies; Thrandur Arnthorsson from
4x4OffRoads.com; Tim Webber – Edale Mountain Rescue; U.S. Coast
Guard; Volvo Car Corporation; Yuba City Police Department

Photograph of Mercedes Benz Unimog SAR Command Vehicle provided
by Galloway Mountain Rescue Team – www.gallowaymrt.org.uk

Photographs by Emily Stone, Patrick Rowe and Kristan Hutchison courtesy
of the National Science Foundation.

CONTENTS

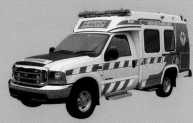

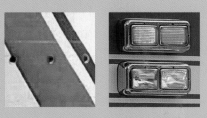

FIRE ENGINES

A fire engine is a big emergency vehicle that puts out fires. It has hoses on board and an extra engine for pumping water. Some fire engines also carry ladders, axes and fire extinguishers. The team of firefighters spray water on the fire.

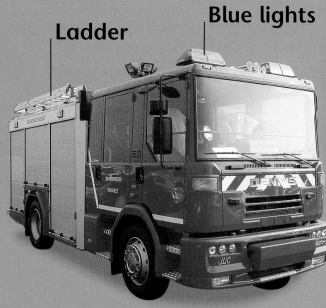

Ladder

Blue lights

Big and bright

Fire engines are big and red so that they are easy to see. This Dennis engine has blue lights on top that flash on and off.

Firefighter

Water power

Most fire engines have room for up to six firefighters on board. One firefighter drives the engine, one firefighter pumps the water and the rest use the hoses.

Can you point to?

a number   some lights   a badge

Huge bumper

Fighting fires

This type of fire engine can put out fires with water, powder and foam. It is used in cities and also for forest fires, and it can easily drive through narrow gaps.

Mega load

The engine below carries 1,892 litres of water. It has enough room on board for six people and lots of equipment.

Special equipment

How many firefighters can you see?

Special dials

Lights

Folded hoses

Locker

FIRE TRUCKS

A fire truck is a rescue vehicle that has ladders, ropes, special tools, a medical kit and rescue equipment on board. A fire truck that also contains a tank of water is called a 'quint'.

Truck with telescopic ladder up

Mega tank

This big fire truck is a quint. It has enough room inside for 10 firefighters and can easily carry 11,356 litres of water in its tanks.

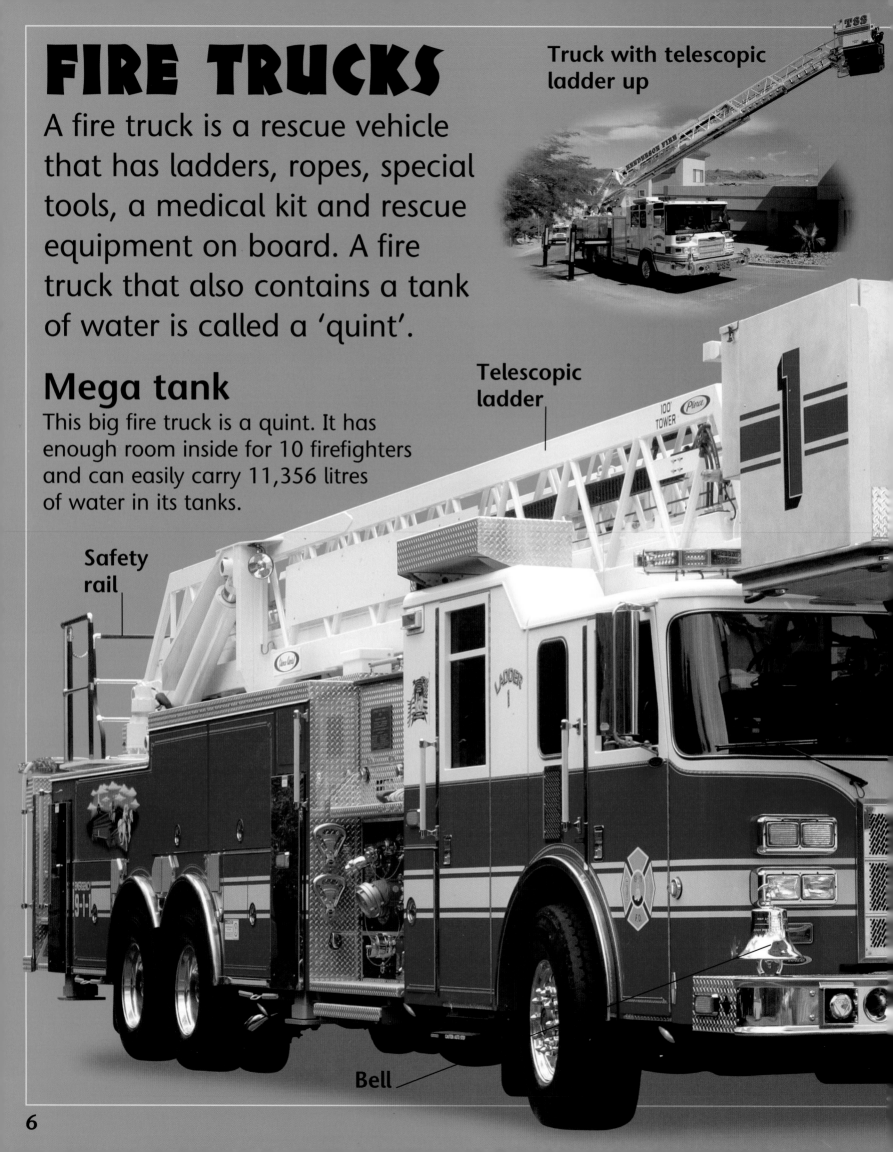

Telescopic ladder

Safety rail

Bell

Safe buildings

This Supervac truck is used in New York, USA. If a building or some scaffolding collapses it races to the rescue. There is lots of special equipment on board.

Foam sprayer

Off-roader

This tough fire truck can drive on rough ground, through mud and up steep slopes to rescue people. The truck's bodywork is high up off the ground.

Can you find a bell anywhere?

Siren

Dangerous materials

The truck above is used when there is an accident with hazardous (dangerous) materials. This truck is full of all sorts of rescue equipment, but it does not carry ladders, water or a hose.

7

AIRPORT RESCUERS

Rescue vehicles at airports need to be tough and fast. They may have to drive over slippery ground or through water. They often have six wheels and are very powerful. They carry water and foam on board, and can put out any kind of aircraft fire.

Red racer

This truck goes from 0 to 50 miles an hour in 25 seconds! It can drive over any kind of surface at an airport.

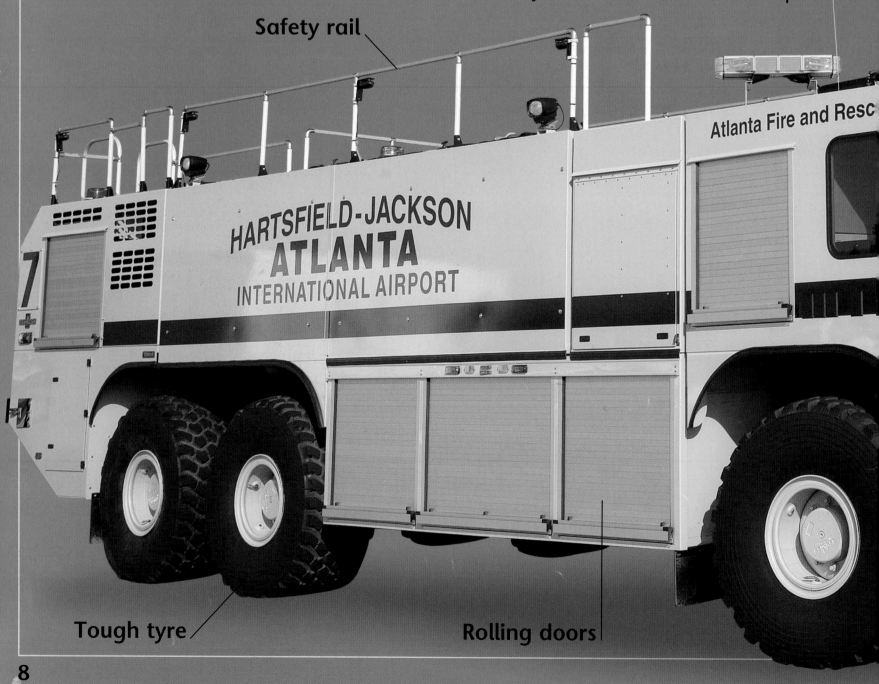

Safety rail

HARTSFIELD-JACKSON **ATLANTA** INTERNATIONAL AIRPORT

Atlanta Fire and Resc

Tough tyre

Rolling doors

Can you point to?

a badge

a number

a foot step

Water pump

Airport truck spraying water

Where can you see a fire?

Big windows

Mega tank

This airport rescuer can carry up to 10,000 litres of water in its tank. It has a 420 horsepower engine, which means it would take 420 horses to pull it along!

Super truck

This truck has big windows to help the driver see clearly. It moves quickly and can climb over low walls and through water. It is called a 'Striker'.

Foot step

Oshkosh® Striker® putting out a fire

9

AMBULANCES

All over the world, these important vehicles rescue people and take them to hospital. Ambulances have loud sirens and flashing lights to tell other traffic to get out of the way. Inside there is space for patients, doctors and emergency equipment.

Six wheels

This special ambulance is used by the British Air Force. It has six wheels and can drive up steep hills and over boggy or rough ground.

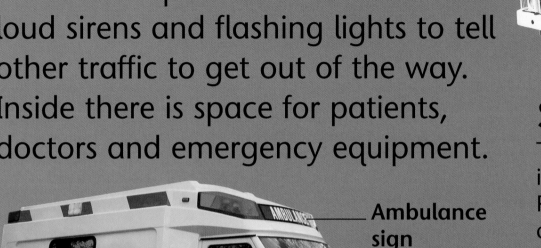

Ambulance sign

Lights

Colourful rescuer

Ambulances are usually yellow and red, or white and red so that people can see them easily. They often have chevrons or other patterns along the sides to make them stand out more.

Which ambulance has six wheels?

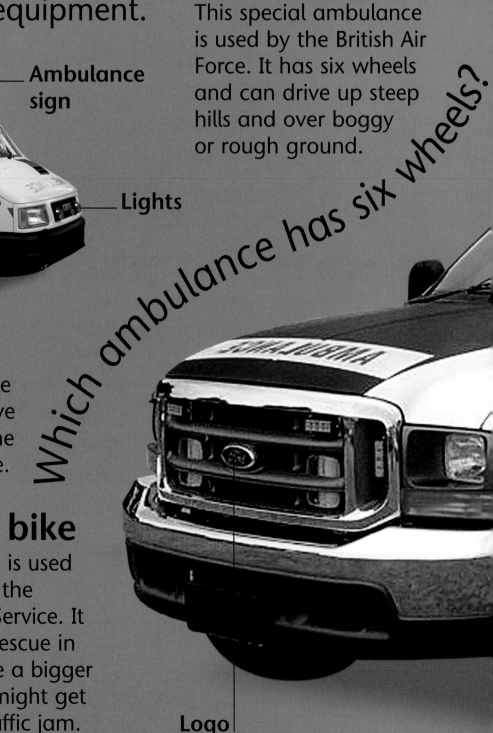

Speedy bike

This fast bike is used in the UK by the Ambulance Service. It goes to the rescue in towns, where a bigger ambulance might get stuck in a traffic jam.

Logo

Can you point to?

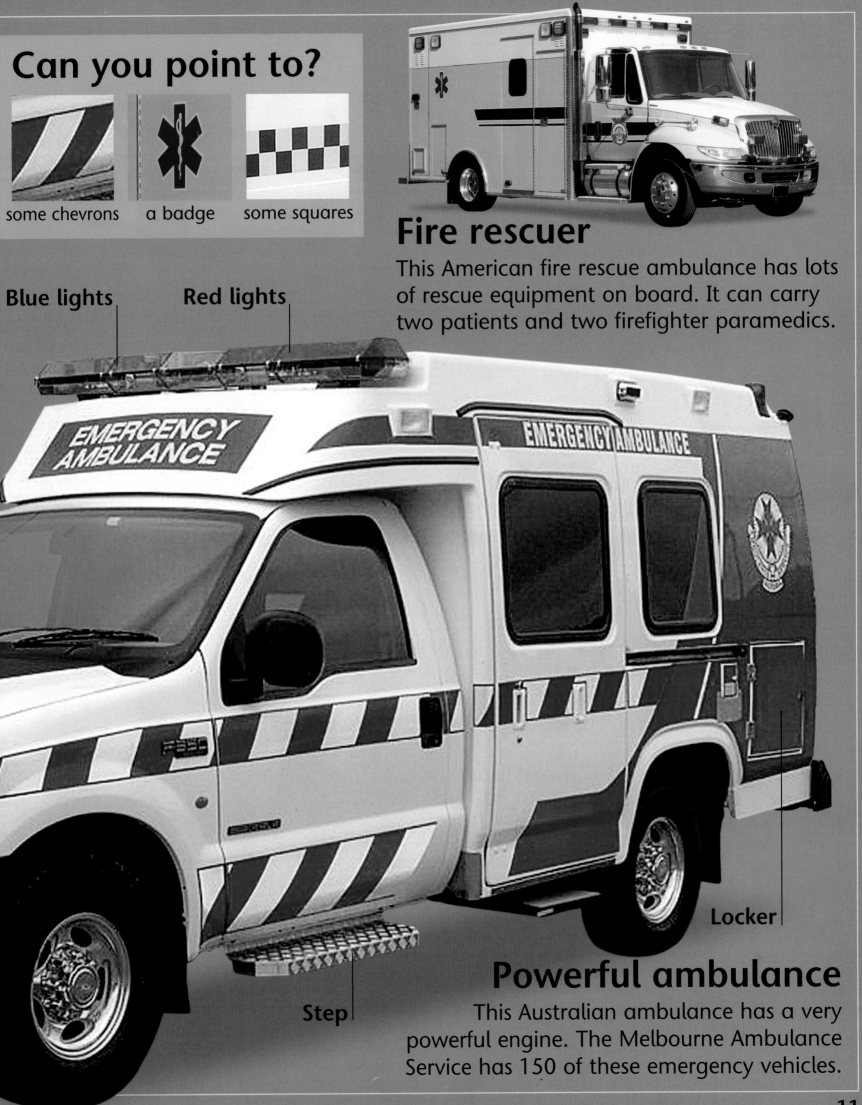

some chevrons

a badge

some squares

Fire rescuer

This American fire rescue ambulance has lots of rescue equipment on board. It can carry two patients and two firefighter paramedics.

Blue lights

Red lights

EMERGENCY AMBULANCE

EMERGENCY AMBULANCE

Locker

Step

Powerful ambulance

This Australian ambulance has a very powerful engine. The Melbourne Ambulance Service has 150 of these emergency vehicles.

POLICE CARS

Police cars do dangerous work so they have to be powerful, tough, fast and safe to drive. A police car has flashing lights and loud sirens to warn other traffic to move out of the way.

Canadian Chevrolet

This police car is used in Canada to patrol the cities and keep them safe. It can go at up to 124 miles an hour!

Chequered pattern

Tough windscreen

Chequered car

In the UK, Volvo police cars have to drive about 60,000 miles every year patrolling roads and motorways. These cars have patterns on them so that other drivers can see them clearly.

Smart car

Smart police car

Little cars like this one are used for lots of jobs, including visiting schools to teach children about police work.

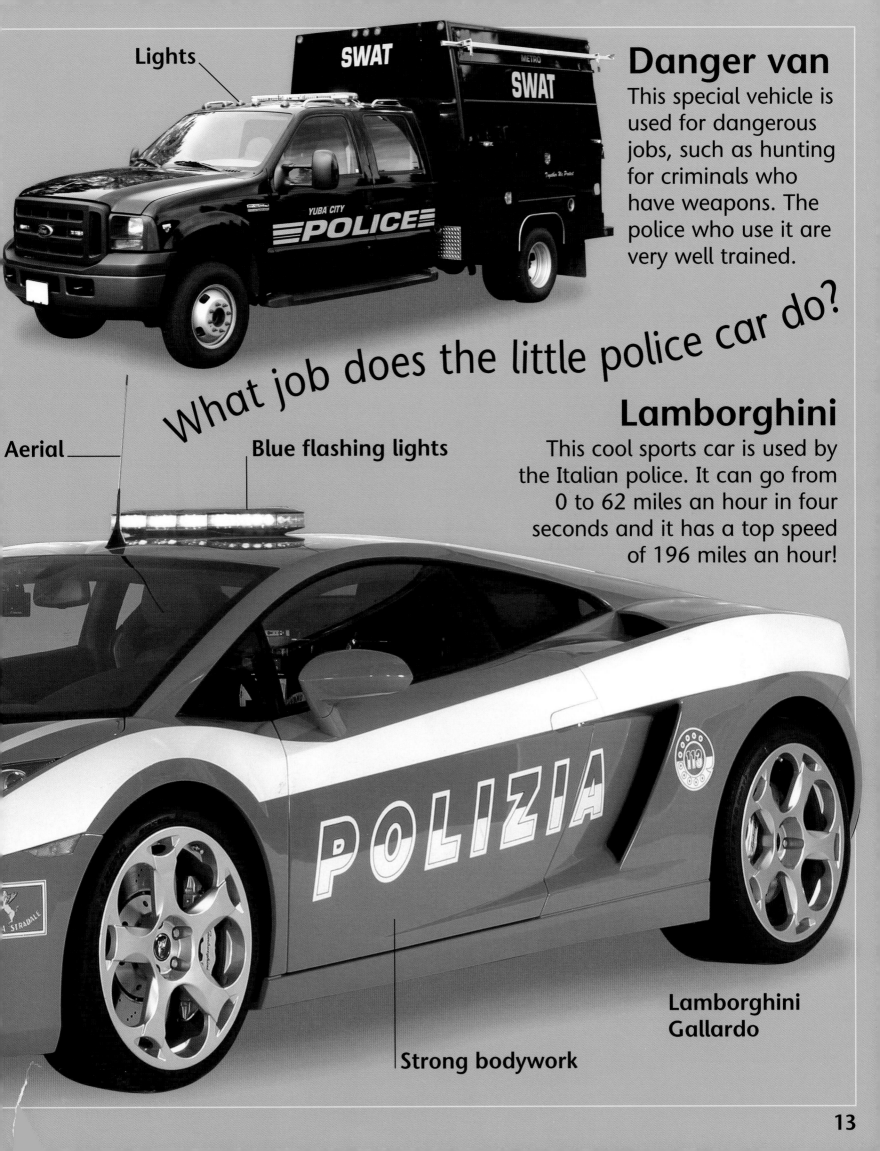

Lights

Danger van

This special vehicle is used for dangerous jobs, such as hunting for criminals who have weapons. The police who use it are very well trained.

SWAT
METRO
SWAT

YUBA CITY
POLICE

What job does the little police car do?

Lamborghini

This cool sports car is used by the Italian police. It can go from 0 to 62 miles an hour in four seconds and it has a top speed of 196 miles an hour!

Aerial

Blue flashing lights

POLIZIA

Lamborghini
Gallardo

Strong bodywork

RECOVERY TRUCKS

When a car, truck or bus breaks down or has a road accident, a recovery truck goes to the rescue. These big, strong vehicles can pick up broken-down vehicles and tow or carry them home.

Can you point to?

a number

a logo

a hubcap

Rescuing a car at the beach

Exhaust

Peterbilt

239-337-5800

USDOT 825704FL

Fuel tank

Grille

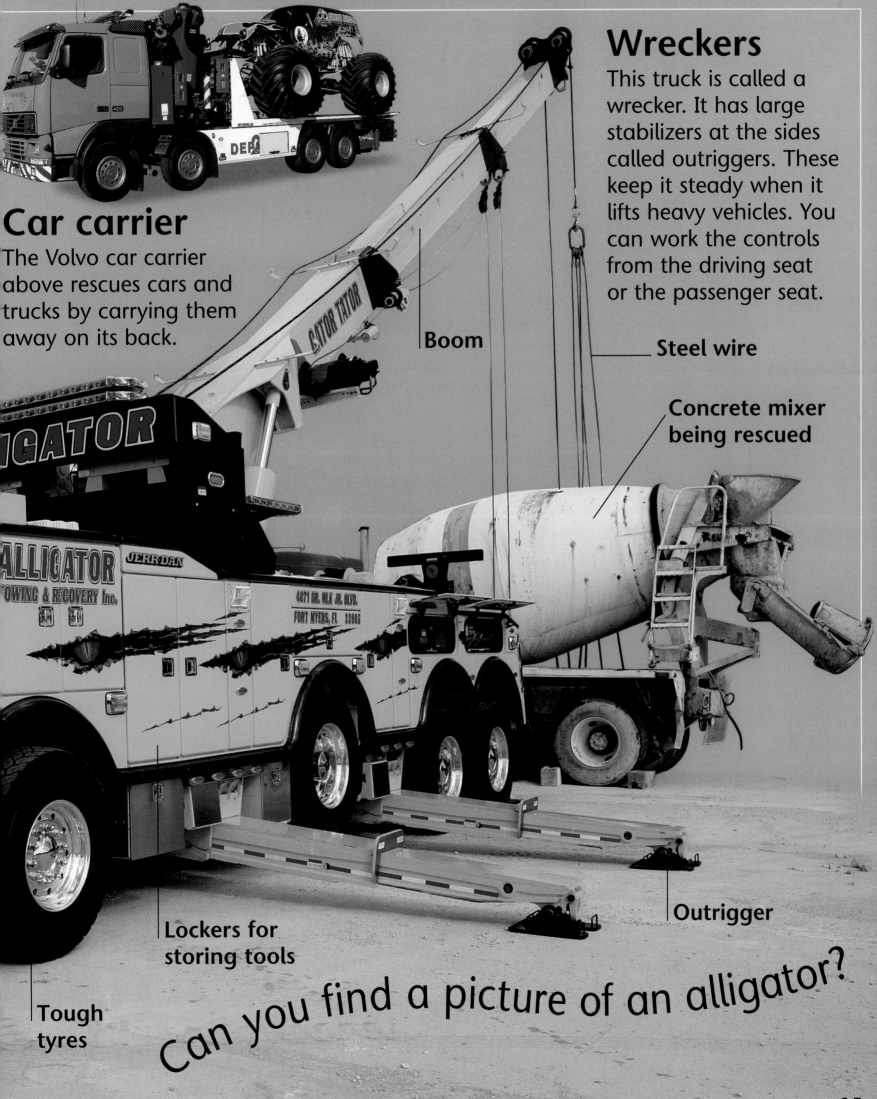

Car carrier

The Volvo car carrier above rescues cars and trucks by carrying them away on its back.

Wreckers

This truck is called a wrecker. It has large stabilizers at the sides called outriggers. These keep it steady when it lifts heavy vehicles. You can work the controls from the driving seat or the passenger seat.

Boom

Steel wire

Concrete mixer being rescued

Lockers for storing tools

Outrigger

Tough tyres

Can you find a picture of an alligator?

SNOW CLEARERS

Fast, powerful snow ploughs, snow blowers and snow brooms keep the roads safe for traffic in winter. These rescue trucks have to work very quickly. They also clear snow off runways at airports.

Tracks

Snow machine

This Snow Cat runs on tracks which help it to drive over the snow. Machines like this one are often used to keep ski runs clear.

Snow broom

This snow broom has two engines. One engine at the back moves the machine forwards and one at the front spins the broom around in the snow.

Exhaust tailpipe

Snow blowers

These snow machines have very powerful engines. Some snow blowers can clear 5,000 tonnes of snow an hour, shooting it out at the sides as they go along. They can throw the snow up to 70 metres away!

Chute

Snow-cutting blades

Which of these snow vehicles drives on tracks?

Cab

Snow plough

Broom

Snow plough

This vehicle's curved plough is seven metres wide. It pushes snow out of the way as it drives. It also pulls along a big broom that sweeps away any snow that is left behind by the large plough.

MOUNTAIN RESCUERS

If someone has an accident on a mountain it is difficult for an ordinary ambulance to reach them. Off-road vehicles can drive up steep hills and rocky tracks to rescue people.

Lots of equipment

Four-by-fours like this Land Rover carry all sorts of equipment, including radios, stretchers, powerful lights, satellite phones and a medical kit.

Stretcher wheel

Stretcher

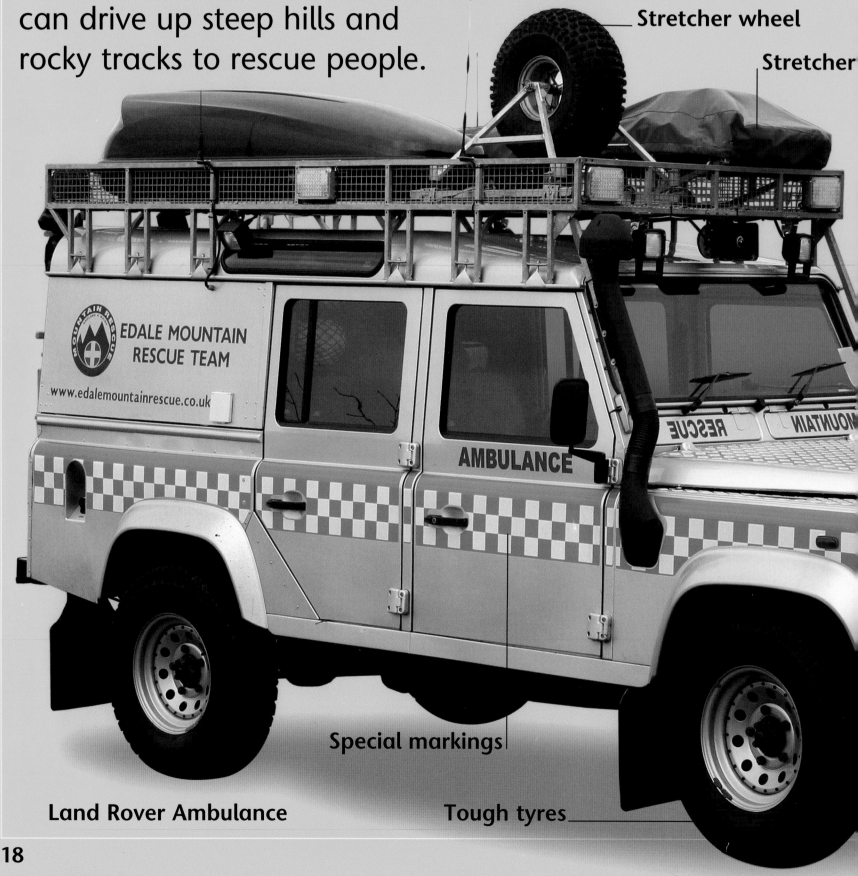

EDALE MOUNTAIN RESCUE TEAM

www.edalemountainrescue.co.uk

AMBULANCE

RESCUE MOUNTAIN

Land Rover Ambulance

Special markings

Tough tyres

Can you point to?

a circle   some squares   a grille

Search light

Aerial

Roof rack

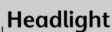

Nissan Patrol

This powerful car is used in snow. It has search lights, a radio, telephone, air tank, cables, a winch, a tow line, stretchers, and avalanche sticks!

Recovery winch

Jeep

The Jeep above can rescue people in deserts as well as up mountains. The roof slides open, the windscreen folds and the doors come off!

Headlight

Can you find a search light?

Blue light

Mountain ambulance

This is a very special kind of ambulance. It has lots of computer equipment inside to help find people when they are lost.

AMAZING RESCUERS

A few rescue vehicles can drive almost anywhere to reach people. They go up mountains or through rivers. Others can drive on snow and ice. Every year, thousands of people are saved by these amazing vehicles.

Going anywhere

The vehicle below drives on rubber tracks. It can go anywhere, even through water. It is so big that it can seat up to 17 people inside!

Snowmobile

This speedy snowmobile has tracks at the back and skis at the front so it can drive over snow and ice. It is often used for rescuing skiers.

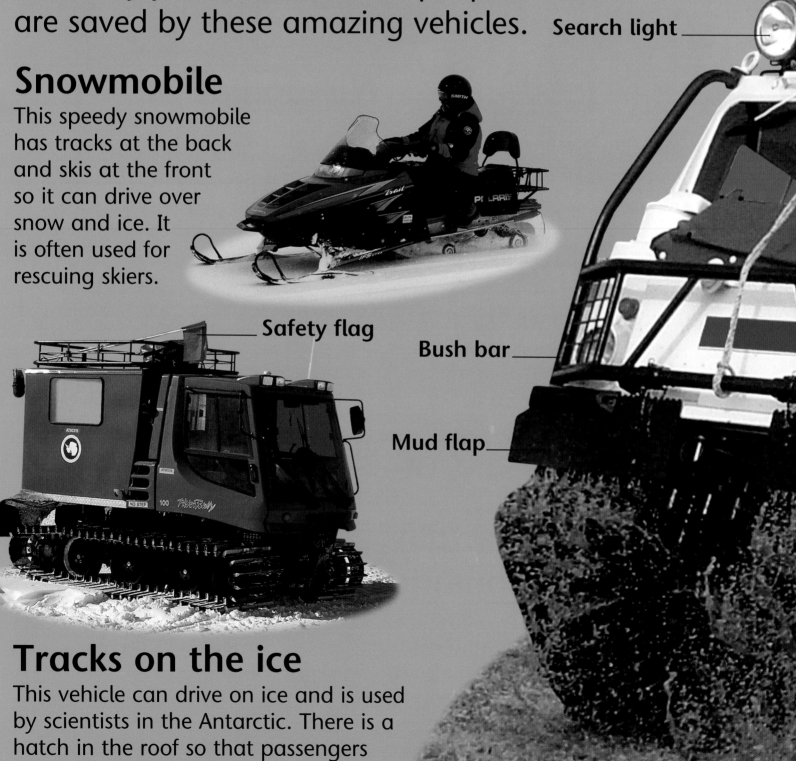

Search light

Safety flag

Bush bar

Mud flap

Tracks on the ice

This vehicle can drive on ice and is used by scientists in the Antarctic. There is a hatch in the roof so that passengers can escape it if falls through the ice.

Can you point to?

a rectangle

a circle

a driver

Quadski going to the rescue

Wheel

Can you find the snowmobile?

Roof rack

Land and sea rescuer

This special quad bike can drive on land and on water. Its four wheels fold up inside, just by flicking a switch! Emergency workers use these machines to rescue people at the seaside.

Rear compartment

ATERV

ALL TERRAIN EMERGENCY RESPONSE VEHICLE

RESCUE HELICOPTERS

Helicopters rescue at sea, on the seashore and up mountains. They are quick and can get to places that other rescuers cannot reach. Helicopters are also used for putting out fires.

Super searcher

Helicopters like this one can carry five tonnes of equipment. They have powerful search lights and carry emergency equipment on board.

Nose

Can you point to the tail rotor?

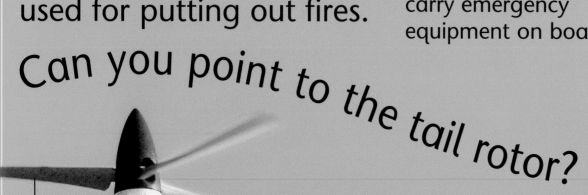

Rotor blade

Wing

Up and away

The helicopter on the left has a hoist on the side so that it can lift people up and away from danger.

Rescuing a person on a stretcher

Mixed up

This rescue aircraft is a mixture of an aeroplane and a helicopter. It can fly in bad weather, and it can also hover. It can fly fast and rescue people far away.

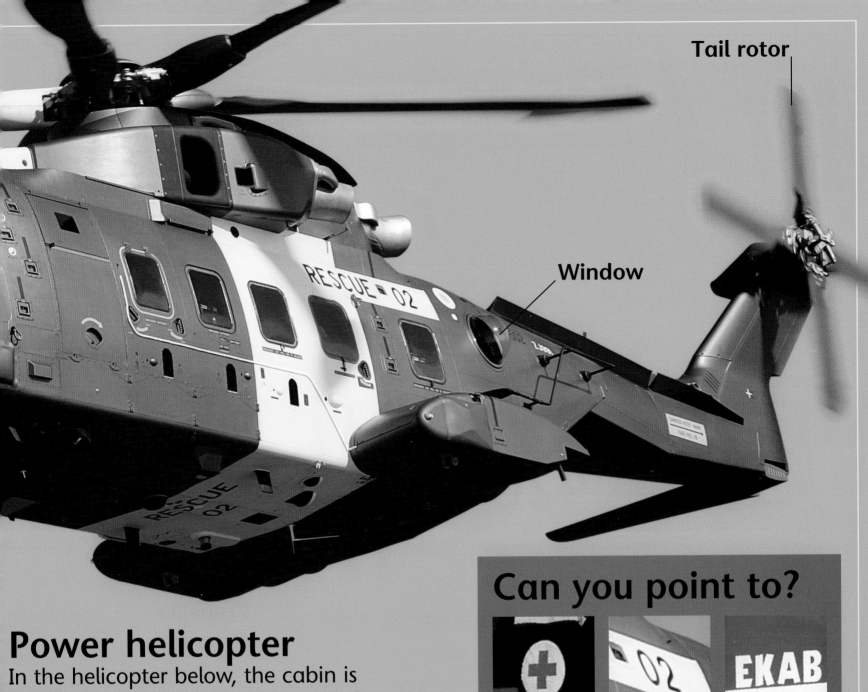

Tail rotor

Window

Power helicopter

In the helicopter below, the cabin is separate from the cockpit. There is lots of space so that doctors can look after patients while the helicopter is flying.

Can you point to?

a cross   a number   some letters

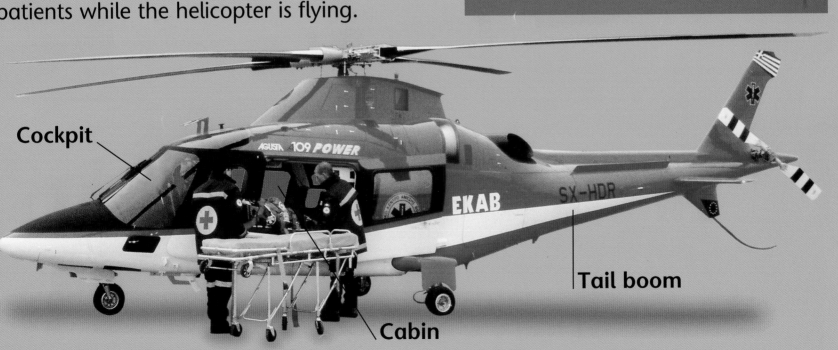

Cockpit

Tail boom

Cabin

AIR TANKERS

In forests and other wild places that fire engines cannot reach, aeroplanes called air tankers carry water and a special liquid for putting out fires. They fly high above the trees, spraying the fire.

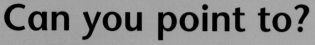

Air tanker putting out a forest fire

Can you point to?

CDF
some letters

some stripes

426
some numbers

Waterbomber

The exciting air tanker above can drop its load from the bottom or the side. It can hold 27,254 litres of liquid and it is the world's largest scooping waterbomber.

Pilot

Propeller

Exhaust

PROPELLER

Engine

Spinner

Cockpit

Wing

Air tractor

This firefighter can fly at 210 miles an hour.
It is useful for putting out fires in small areas.
Aeroplanes like this one are also used for spraying
farm crops, so they are also called air tractors.

Super tanker

The air tanker below is an amazing fire
fighter. It is used for putting out fires in
forests and in the countryside. It flies
at up to 270 miles an hour and carries
4,542 litres of liquid for fighting fires.

CDF

88

Rudder

Stabilizer

N426DF

HOT LOAD

Can you point to the pilot?

FIREBOATS

A fireboat is like a fire engine on water. It has pumps that suck in water and then shoot it out to fight fires on sailing boats and ships. Fireboats carry lots of special fire and rescue equipment on board.

Safety rail

River rescuer

Small fireboats like this one can travel up narrow rivers to put out fires on other boats. This Firestorm boat goes at 43 miles an hour, and pumps thousands of litres of water every minute.

Can you see a funnel?

Firestorm boat

This tough Firestorm fireboat has emergency lights, a fog horn and a siren. There is also a room in the cabin for treating people who are being rescued.

Firestorm fireboat putting out a fire

Water pump

Cabin

NASHVILLE FIRE DEPARTMENT

Hull

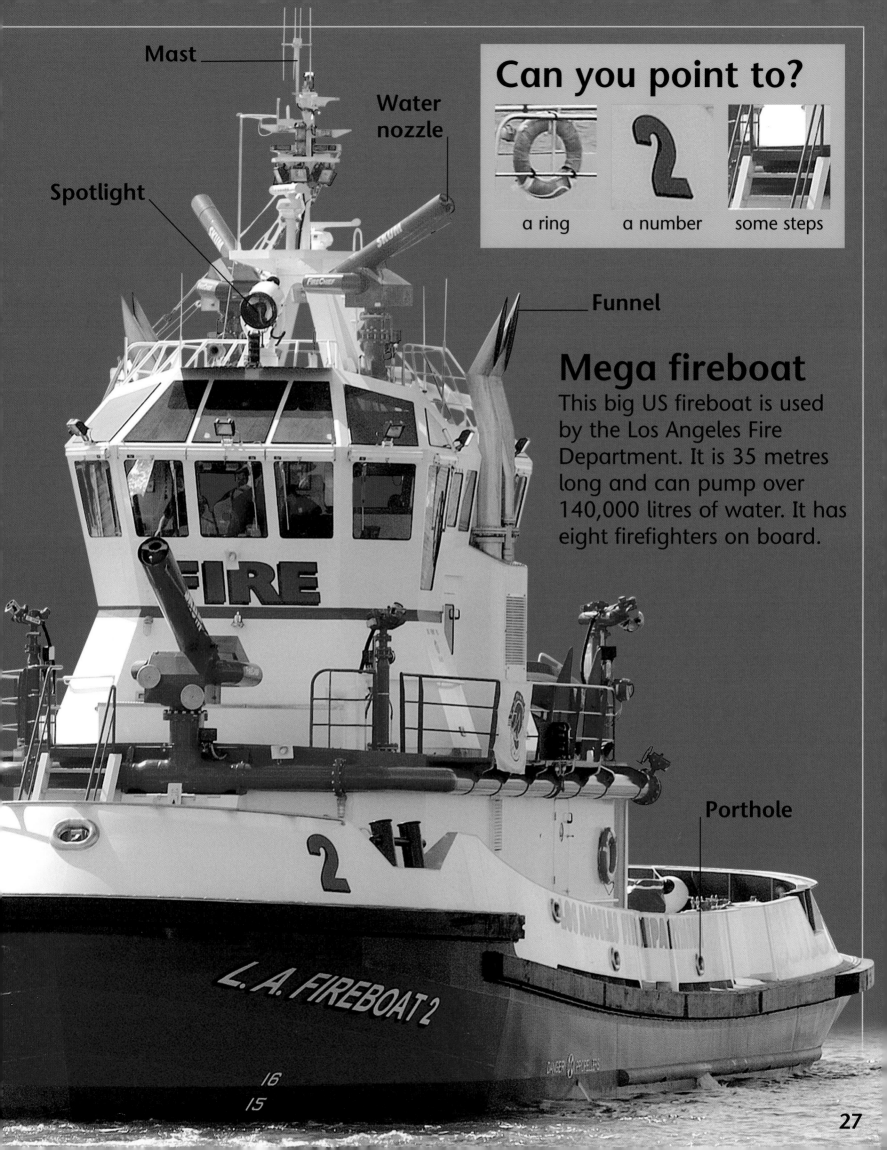

Mast

Water nozzle

Spotlight

Can you point to?

a ring

a number

some steps

Funnel

Mega fireboat

This big US fireboat is used by the Los Angeles Fire Department. It is 35 metres long and can pump over 140,000 litres of water. It has eight firefighters on board.

Porthole

FIRE

2

L.A. FIREBOAT 2

16
15

SEA RESCUERS

Lifeboats rescue people on boats out at sea. They often have to go out in a storm, so the work is very dangerous for the crew. Lifeboats are fast, tough and powerful.

A boat that hovers

A hovercraft glides easily over water, sand and mud, so it is useful for searching along the seashore. At the back are two fans that work like aeroplane propellers.

Water stretcher

The yellow rescue boat above is a blow-up stretcher that floats on water. It used in the sea, and on lakes, rivers, ice and snow.

Fan

DANGER PROPELLERS

RNLI

H-004

Twin outboard engines

Rigid inflatable boat

These powerful boats are also known as RIBs. They are strong and stable and can go fast, even in rough seas. This one has two big engines.

Mast

What colour is the hovercraft?

Window

Safety rail

47206   U.S. COAST GUARD

Strong hull

Motor lifeboat

The amazing motorboat above is used for rescuing people at sea in very bad weather. It is almost unsinkable and can turn itself upright in less than 30 seconds!

Sea searcher

Over 300 of these boats are used by the US Coastguard to rescue people. They can travel in rough seas with waves up to three metres high!

251058   COAST GUARD

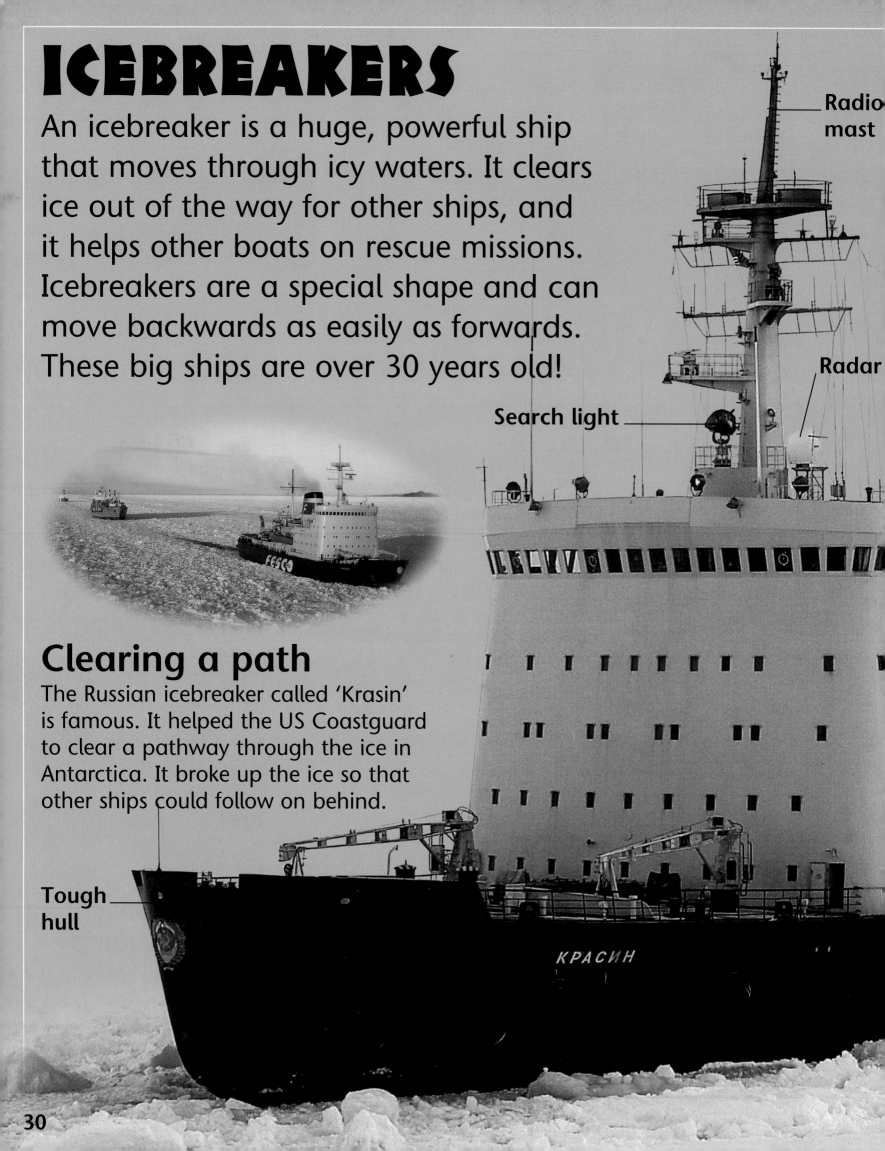

ICEBREAKERS

An icebreaker is a huge, powerful ship that moves through icy waters. It clears ice out of the way for other ships, and it helps other boats on rescue missions. Icebreakers are a special shape and can move backwards as easily as forwards. These big ships are over 30 years old!

Radio mast

Radar

Search light

Clearing a path

The Russian icebreaker called 'Krasin' is famous. It helped the US Coastguard to clear a pathway through the ice in Antarctica. It broke up the ice so that other ships could follow on behind.

Tough hull

КРАСИН

Mega icebreaker

This US icebreaker is called the 'Polar Sea'. There is room for 20 scientists and two helicopters on board. It also has a shop and a library. The 'Polar Sea' can push through ice six metres thick!

Crane

Anchor

U.S. COAST GUARD

11

Funnel

Mast

IMO 7359644

FESCO

Can you point to?

a letter

a lifeboat

a flag

Super ship

An icebreaker is very strong. Propellers at the front and back push the ship forwards. The ship drives on to the ice and is so heavy that the ice breaks underneath it.

What job does an icebreaker do?

LET'S MATCH!

Can you find all the matching pairs on this page?
Where is the yellow helicopter?

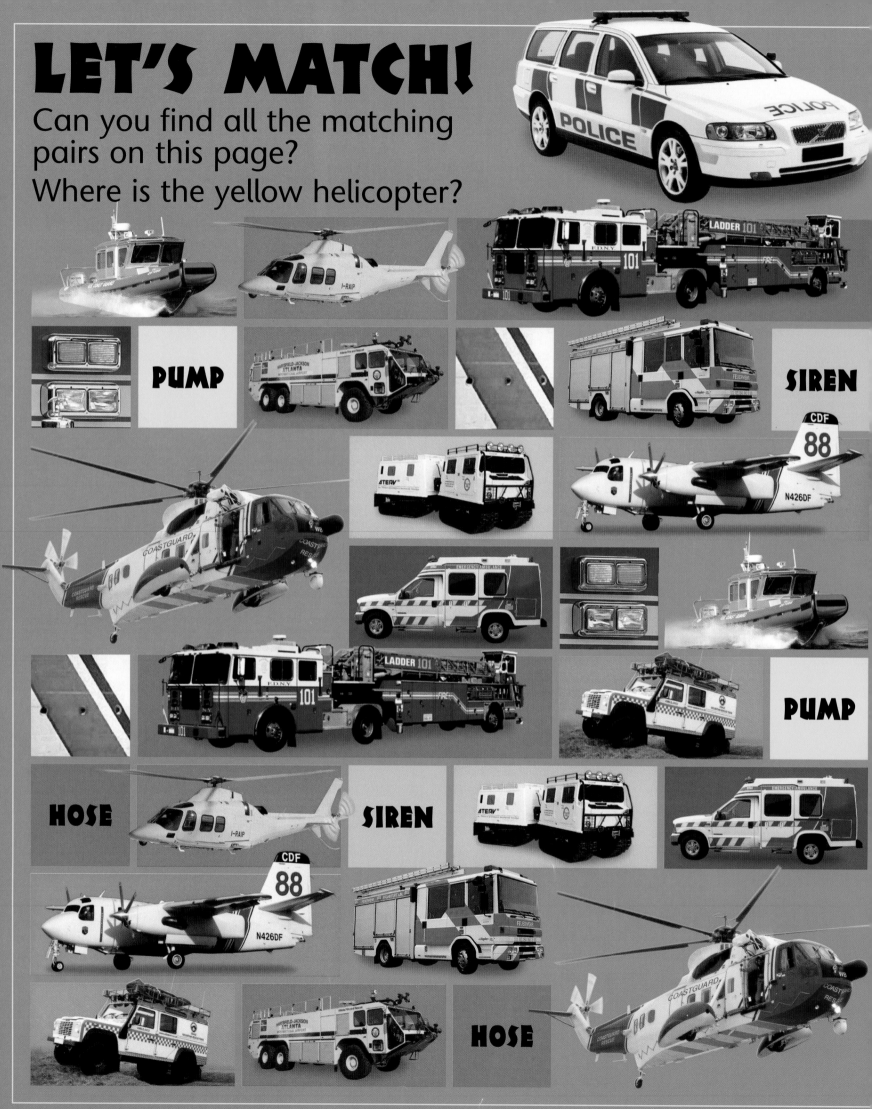

PUMP

SIREN

HOSE

SIREN

PUMP

HOSE